10 GOALS

10 GREEN GOALS

JANE BURNARD • FATTI BURKE

PowerKiDS press

Published in 2027
by The Rosen Publishing Group, Inc.
2544 Clinton Street, Buffalo, NY 14224

First published in Great Britain in 2022 by Wayland

Credits

Editor: Julia Bird

Editorial, design and project management: Raspberry Books

Design: Intrepid Books LTD

Illustrations: Fatti Burke

Cataloging-in-Publication Data

Names: Burnard, Jane, author. | Burke, Fatti, illustrator.
Title: 10 green goals / written by Jane Burnard, illustrated by Fatti Burke.
Description: Buffalo, New York : PowerKids Press, 2027. | Series: 10 goals | Includes glossary and index.
Identifiers: ISBN 9781499459098 (pbk.) | ISBN 9781499459104 (library bound) | ISBN 9781499459111 (ebook)
Subjects: LCSH: Green movement--Juvenile literature. | Sustainable living--Juvenile literature. | Environmentalism--Juvenile literature.
Classification: LCC GE195.5 B876 2027 | DDC 640.286--dc23

Printed in China

CPSIA Compliance Information: Batch #QS27PK. For further information contact Rosen Publishing at 1-800-237-9932.

CONTENTS

WHY GREEN GOALS ARE GOOD

Do you want to achieve 10 goals to make planet Earth a better place? Then read on.

First the bad news. Our planet's in trouble, because of the way we live. We're fast using up the world's natural resources and damaging it with pollution. We produce greenhouse gases (such as carbon dioxide) when we travel, heat our homes, and make things in factories. These greenhouse gases trap energy from the sun, causing our planet to heat up. This is called global warming, and it's causing increasing temperatures, rising sea levels, storms, floods and drought all over the world.

But here's the good news! There's loads we can do to help the planet, right here and now. If we all work together, we really can make a difference. And reading this book is a great first step.

GOAL 1

EAT GREENER

Whether you're a meat-eater, a vegetarian, or a vegan, find out some food facts and decide whether you need to change the way you eat.

Don't worry – you can still enjoy your food and protect the planet at the same time!

EVERY TWO SECONDS, A FOOTBALL-FIELD-SIZED AREA OF RAINFOREST IS BURNED DOWN TO MAKE WAY FOR FOOD PRODUCTION. THE PRECIOUS AMAZON RAINFOREST IS BEING CLEARED FOR GRAZING BEEF CATTLE AND PLANTATIONS OF SOYBEANS TO FEED THE CHICKENS, PIGS, AND FISH WE EAT.

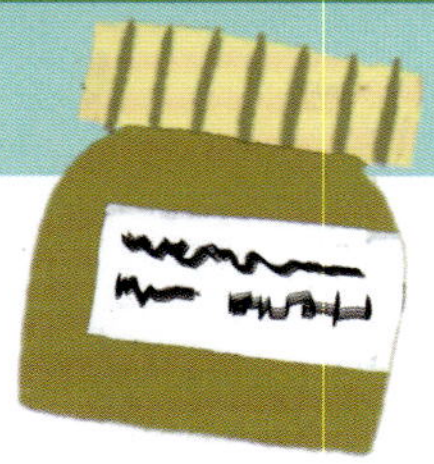

Globally, nearly half of all packaged food contains palm oil. The forests of Southeast Asia, habitat of endangered orangutans, are being destroyed to create ever more palm oil plantations.

Food is often transported hundreds of "food miles" by trucks, ships, or airplanes before it reaches our plates.

When it rots, food produces huge amounts of methane, a **GREENHOUSE GAS.**

AROUND 1.4 MILLION TONS (1.3 MT) OF THE WORLD'S EDIBLE FOOD GETS THROWN AWAY EVERY YEAR, WHILE ONE IN NINE PEOPLE DON'T HAVE ENOUGH TO EAT.

Producing just one kilogram of beef creates a whopping 37 times more carbon dioxide than growing the same amount of beans, lentils, or tofu.

TOP TIPS TO REACH

There's enough food in the world to feed us all, if we treat our environment with respect. Here's how to lessen your impact on our planet and enjoy a tastier, healthier diet:

1 EAT FEWER ANIMALS AND MORE PLANTS

NO ONE NEEDS TO EAT MEAT OR FISH EVERY DAY. FRESH FRUIT AND VEGETABLES ARE FULL OF VITAMINS, AND THERE'S LOADS OF PROTEIN IN NUTS, BEANS, LENTILS, AND BREAD. WHAT ABOUT A MEAT-FREE MONDAY? OR JUST HAVING MEAT ON SPECIAL OCCASIONS? YOU COULD CUT DOWN ON EGGS, MILK, AND CHEESE TOO.

2 CHECK FOOD LABELS

Make sure that the palm oil in anything you buy is RSPO (Roundtable on Sustainable Palm Oil) certified, which means it comes from a plantation that puts the wellbeing of nature and people first. Look out for a blue Marine Stewardship Council logo on fish packaging, which is better for our oceans. Organic meat, vegetables, and fruit are produced in ways that are better for the planet and kinder to animals.

YOUR GREEN FOOD GOAL

3 DON'T THROW FOOD AWAY

STOP FOOD WASTE. IF YOU CAN'T EAT WHAT'S ON YOUR PLATE, PUT IT IN THE FREEZER.

4 EAT LOCAL FOOD

This means buying food that's grown and produced as close to where you live as possible – to save on food miles.

5 GROW YOUR OWN FOOD

IT'S FUN – AND A GREAT WAY TO AVOID FOOD MILES. WHY NOT START WITH VITAMIN-FILLED RADISHES – THEY'RE QUICK AND EASY TO GROW. YOU CAN EVEN GROW THEM IN A POT!

HAPPY EATING!

What are YOU wearing right now?

Are your clothes:

a) old and mended,

or

b) brand new, ready to be thrown away when they're in danger of going out of fashion?

If you answered a), you're already on your way to achieving this goal. If you answered b), it's time to rethink your wardrobe.

GOAL 2

CUT DOWN ON CLOTHES

(and Other Things Too)

More and more people are buying cheap clothes, wearing them once or twice, then throwing them away and buying new ones. But as well as the price tag you see in the shop, there are hidden costs that the planet ends up paying.

Clothes are made in factories, and most are powered by fossil fuels (see page 34).

MAKING CLOTHES PRODUCES A LOT OF WASTE MATERIAL.

Dyeing cloth is a major cause of water pollution.

Producing just one pair of jeans uses 1,981 gallons (7,500 l) of water!

Making clothes uses more water than any other industry except farming.

TEXTILES SUCH AS POLYESTER RELEASE TINY PARTICLES OF PLASTIC, WHICH EVENTUALLY FIND THEIR WAY INTO THE OCEAN.

Millions of tons of clothing end up rotting away on trash dumps every year.

TOP TIPS TO CUT

You can't stop yourself from growing out of your old clothes, but that doesn't mean you always have to buy brand new ones. Here are some simple ways to help you achieve this green goal:

1 THROW A CLOTHES-SWAPPING PARTY

The clothes might not be new, but they're new to you! Swapping with your friends makes a change from family hand-me-downs.

2 GO THRIFT SHOPPING

TAKE YOUR PARENT OR CARER SHOPPING IN THRIFT OR VINTAGE SHOPS – FINDING FASHION BARGAINS CAN BE FUN AND YOU'LL BE HELPING THE ENVIRONMENT AT THE SAME TIME.

DOWN ON CLOTHES

3 GET CREATIVE

When your clothes are a bit worn out, you could just mend them (find out how to sew seams and attach buttons if you don't already know). But you could also let your artistic side loose! Make a pair of old jeans into shorts, or customize a T-shirt.

In your bid to buy fewer new clothes, you will be doing the world a lot of good.

DON'T STOP THERE, THOUGH! THINK BEFORE ASKING FOR ANYTHING NEW – DO YOU REALLY NEED IT? WHENEVER SOMETHING IS MADE NEW, FROM A PHONE TO A BICYCLE, IT USES ENERGY AND RESOURCES, SO SECONDHAND IS ALWAYS BETTER.

GOAL 3

REDUCE, REUSE, RECYCLE

When you've finished with something, what do you do with it? Chuck it in the trash? Read this, and, next time, stop and think.

Advertising encourages us to buy ever more new things – such as toys, computer games, and phones. Factories produce them, giving off greenhouse gases. Then we throw them out and buy newer things. It's an endless cycle.

The world produces at least 55 tons (50 tonnes) of household waste every single second. In Europe the average person throws out 1,047 pounds (475 kg) of trash a year, the weight of a small car. In North America it's 1,642 pounds (745 kg.)

Most countries recycle materials such as metal, glass, wood, paper, and some plastics – but most trash is buried in landfills or burned.

BURNING WASTE ADDS TO THE PROBLEM OF AIR POLLUTION AND PRODUCES 5 PERCENT OF THE WORLD'S CARBON DIOXIDE EMISSIONS – MAKING THE CLIMATE CRISIS EVEN WORSE.

Most of our waste is made up of organic materials, such as kitchen waste. When this breaks down into compost, it's good for your garden. But most organic waste goes into landfill, where it can't do any good.

Some zero-waste heroes can fit their whole year's trash in a large jar! How small can you make yours?

TOP TIPS TO REDUCE,

To reduce the world's gigantic trash heap we need to 1) buy less, 2) reuse more and 3) recycle more – that means using things for as long as possible, then finding other uses for them. Here's how!

Reducing what we buy is the most important tip!

1 BUY LESS

Reduce how much you buy in the first place. And when you have to buy new, go for good quality and look after your things so that they last.

2 REUSE WORN-OUT ITEMS

GET CREATIVE AND MAKE NEW THINGS OUT OF OLD! YOU COULD MAKE RAG RUGS FROM WORN-OUT T-SHIRTS OR WIND CHIMES, PLANTERS, AND BIRD FEEDERS FROM OLD TIN CANS AND PLASTIC BOTTLES.

REUSE AND RECYCLE

3 DONATE YOUR OLD STUFF

Help the planet by keeping the things we use and wear in circulation, not in landfill. Give unwanted items to secondhand shops, or sell them at a garage sale.

4 RECYCLE AS MUCH AS YOU CAN

BECOME YOUR FAMILY'S RECYCLING MONITOR! CHECK WITH YOUR LOCAL AUTHORITY TO FIND OUT WHAT THEY CAN AND CAN'T RECYCLE, THEN DON'T LET ANYTHING RECYCLABLE GO INTO THE TRASH BIN.

5 COMPOST ORGANIC WASTE

Organic waste is waste that comes from plants or animals, and includes vegetable peels, used teabags, and eggshells. If you have a garden, put organic waste in a compost bin, where it can rot down to make food for the soil. (Ask an adult to help you buy or make a compost bin if you don't have one.) Or put it in your local community's organic waste recycling bins.

Reducing and reusing are the very best ways to stop adding to the trash mountain.

GOAL 4

USE LESS PLASTIC

Plastic is all around us – from the deepest depths of our oceans to the summit of Mount Everest. Tiny plastic particles even float in the air we breathe. What can you do to make sure you don't add to the world's plastic pollution?

Nine million tons of plastic waste ends up in the oceans every year. That's the equivalent of FIVE rows of shopping bags, full of plastic, piled up around the whole of the world's coastlines.

Turtles, fish and seabirds can mistake plastic for food, eat it, and die. Microplastics (tiny, broken-down pieces of plastic) lodge in the bodies of microscopic sea creatures and enter the food chain as bigger animals eat them.

Forty percent of plastic pollution is single-use plastic, which is packaging used once and then discarded. On average, one person throws away 307 plastic bags per year in the United States alone, while nearly a million plastic drink bottles are sold every minute around the world.

LESS THAN TWENTY PERCENT OF ALL PLASTIC IS RECYCLED GLOBALLY – THE REST GOES TO LANDFILL, IS BURNED, OR LITTERS THE LAND AND THE SEA. SOME PLASTICS ARE IMPOSSIBLE TO RECYCLE.

Plastic is made from oil and natural gases, which are fossil fuels (see page 34). Making plastic creates greenhouse gases.

TOP TIPS TO USE

Do we want to live on a plastic planet?
NO! The revolution starts here.

1 AVOID SINGLE-USE PLASTIC

CARRY A REUSABLE SHOPPING BAG AND ASK YOUR PARENT OR CARER TO BUY LOOSE, UNWRAPPED FOOD WHENEVER POSSIBLE. SUGGEST BUYING LAUNDRY POWDER AND BARS OF SOAP IN CARDBOARD BOXES, RATHER THAN AS LIQUID IN PLASTIC BOTTLES, AND SWITCH TO BAMBOO TOOTHBRUSHES.

2 EAT PLASTIC-FREE SNACKS

Pack sandwiches and snacks in reusable containers or cloth sacks instead of plastic bags. Snack on fruit instead of plastic-wrapped treats, chips, and candy bars – it's much healthier too!

3 DON'T BUY DRINKS IN PLASTIC BOTTLES

TAKE WATER AND OTHER DRINKS WITH YOU IN A REUSABLE METAL BOTTLE.

LESS PLASTIC

4 THROW A PLASTIC-FREE PARTY

THIS IS A GREAT WAY TO LET FAMILY AND FRIENDS KNOW ABOUT THE PLASTIC PROBLEM. SAY NO TO BALLOONS (MARINE ANIMALS MISTAKE THEM FOR FOOD). INSTEAD, CUT OUT PAPER DECORATIONS SUCH AS BUNTING, STREAMERS, AND CONFETTI. BAN GLITTER (IT'S TINY PIECES OF PLASTIC). USE PAPER STRAWS FOR DRINKS.

5 RECYCLE!

Recycle as much plastic as you can – better still, don't buy plastic you will need to throw away any time soon!

By saying no to plastic, you're sending a strong message to shops. When we refuse to buy plastic packaging, eventually they'll stop selling it to us.

GOAL 5

HELP NATURE

Nature is good for us! Studies show that regular visits to the countryside and activities such as gardening and feeding birds make us feel ↕ calmer, happier, and healthier. And the natural world also provides us with fresh air, food, and medicine.

HOWEVER ...
As the world's population grows, our actions are damaging insects, birds, and mammals. We're harming their homes, taking their food, and destroying them by:

- CLEARING THE COUNTRYSIDE TO BUILD MORE HOUSES AND ROADS.
- Burning forests and draining wetlands to grow crops.
- Taking fresh water from rivers and springs.
- POLLUTING THE SEA AND LAND WITH PLASTIC AND PESTICIDES.
- Overfishing and overhunting wild fish and animals.

When your grandparents were your age, there were two-thirds more wild mammals, birds, freshwater fish, reptiles, and amphibians than there are now. And insects, such as the bees and moths that pollinate the plants we eat, are declining in numbers too.

BUT WE CAN TAKE STEPS TO PROTECT, RESPECT, AND RESTORE THE PLANET THAT IS HOME TO ALL OF US.

TOP TIPS TO HELP NATURE

Here's how we can help nature, starting in our own backyards!

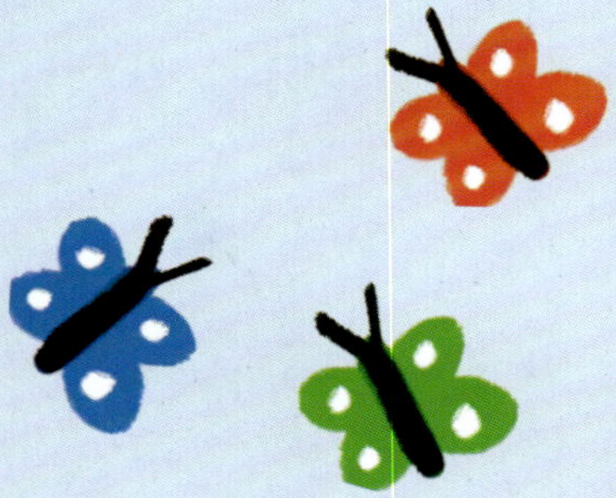

1 LOOK AFTER YOUR OWN GREEN SPACES

Get outside, enjoy and protect the green spaces around you – whether that's your garden, a park, or the local countryside.

2 PICK UP LITTER

GET YOUR FRIENDS TO HELP – IT DOESN'T SOUND LIKE MUCH FUN, BUT IT IS! FIND OUT IF YOU CAN TAKE PART IN A BEACH CLEAN-UP, TOO.

NURTURE NATURE!

3 MAKE A BUG HOTEL

Give insects a safe place to rest and shelter. Bug hotels are easy to make – look for instructions on the internet.

5 PLANT SOME INSECT-FRIENDLY FLOWERS

Many insects, including bees, enjoy feeding on flower nectar. Give them a treat by growing nectar-rich flowers in your garden, a pot, or a window box.

4 HELP BIRDS

BIRDS LOVE TO BATHE AND NEED TO DRINK THROUGHOUT THE YEAR. HELP THEM BY LEAVING OUT A SHALLOW DISH OF WATER, KEEPING IT CLEAN AND TOPPING IT UP. HANG UP A BIRD FEEDER OR TWO, AND SEE WHO COMES FOR LUNCH! BIRDS ALSO NEED HOMES TO NEST IN. ASK AN ADULT TO HELP YOU ATTACH A BIRD BOX TO YOUR HOME.

Remember – we're all part of the natural world. So when we help and look after wildlife and plants, we're doing ourselves good too.

GOAL 6

PLANT A TREE

(OR GET MORE PLANTED IN YOUR AREA)

Trees do so much good for the planet, but right now they need help. And that's where you come in!

TREES ABSORB CARBON DIOXIDE (A GREENHOUSE GAS) AND GIVE OUT OXYGEN. THEY STORE CARBON IN THEIR WOOD, SLOWING THE RATE OF GLOBAL WARMING.

Trees provide shade on a sunny day, reduce noise and wind, and cool the air as they lose moisture and reflect heat up from their leaves. They can reduce temperatures in sweltering cities by up to 45 °F (7 °C)!

The leaves of just a single tree can filter out up to 3.7 pounds (1.7 kg) of dust and air-pollution particles.

Trees provide fruit, nuts, and other food. They help prevent flooding by absorbing thousands of gallons (litres) of stormwater, and their roots hold the soil together, stopping erosion.

OVER 42 MILLION TREES ARE DESTROYED EVERY SINGLE DAY – CUT DOWN FOR TIMBER OR FUEL, OR BURNED TO MAKE WAY FOR AGRICULTURE.

Trees are sometimes called the lungs of the Earth. Let's help the planet breathe and get planting!

TOP TIPS TO CARE

Plant a tree for PLANET EARTH!

1 FIND THE RIGHT TREE

If you have a garden, ask your parent or carer if you can plant a tree in it. Then get advice – you don't want a giant redwood in a tiny garden! Some small trees can be grown in pots. If you can't do that, try tip number 2!

2 JOIN A TREE-PLANTING PROJECT

VOLUNTEER WITH A LOCAL NATURE ORGANIZATION TO PLANT TREES IN PUBLIC AREAS.

FOR TREES

3 BECOME YOUR TREE'S BEST FRIEND

Trees are like people – they need care when they're young, but when they're grown up they can look after themselves – and you. Watch to see that the tree or trees you helped plant are healthy, follow advice and take special care to keep them watered as they start out. Visit your tree as often as you can. Trees have other visitors too – watch out for insects, birds, and small mammals!

You've just done something wonderful for the planet. You've planted something for yourself and for people in the future, because trees usually live longer than we do. A Great Basin bristlecone pine in the White Mountains of California is believed to be over 5,000 years old!

GOAL 7

SAVE WATER

Did you know that when you flushed the toilet and showered this morning, you were using the world's most precious resource – fresh water?

CouldYOU help the planet by using less of it?

Only 3 percent of the world's water is fresh. And two-thirds of that can't be used because it's frozen into glaciers or deep underground.

The average person in Africa uses 12 gallons (47 l) of water a day. In Europe it's 38gallons (144 l) and it's 153 gallons (578 l) in the United States.

As the world's population grows, we drain more and more water from rivers, underground rocks, and lakes, damaging natural habitats. More than half of the world's wetlands have disappeared.

WE NEED TO DRINK WATER TO SURVIVE. WE ALSO NEED IT FOR WATERING THE PLANTS THAT WE EAT AND WASHING.

Some of us are lucky – we have clean water on tap. But 2.4 billion people live where water is scarce and 2 million people, mostly children, die each year because of disease due to unclean water.

NINETY-TWO PERCENT OF THE WORLD'S AVAILABLE FRESH WATER IS USED IN FACTORIES, POWER PLANTS, SHOPS, AND FOR FARMING. SO WHEN WE BUY MORE NEW THINGS, WE'RE ALSO USING UP A LOT OF WATER.

Drop by drop, we're draining the planet dry. Let's look after our precious water, and start saving it instead.

TOP TIPS TO SAVE WATER

Water experts say that we all need to cut down our water use to 21 gallons (80 l) or less each day. But:

1 person's drinking for one day = 2 litres
Washing face and brushing teeth = 3 litres
1 flush of toilet = 9 litres
5-minute shower = 50 litres

That's 64 litres, about 20 gallons, already! Thankfully, there's loads we can do to save water while still doing everything we need to. Here are some top tips:

1 TURN OFF THE TAP

... while brushing your teeth and washing your hands.

2 TAKE SHORT SHOWERS INSTEAD OF BATHS

A BATH USES 75 PERCENT MORE WATER THAN A FIVE-MINUTE SHOWER!

3 DON'T FLUSH EVERY TIME YOU USE THE TOILET AT HOME

IN OTHER WORDS, DON'T FLUSH THE TOILET WHEN YOU'VE ONLY HAD A PEE!

4 BE A WATER MONITOR

Check taps to see if they're dripping, then tell an adult so they get fixed. Just one drop every second adds up to nearly 6 gallons (23 l) a day, wasted down the drain! You can also catch water in a bowl when you're waiting for it to run hot, then use it on the garden.

5 COLLECT RAINWATER

HELP A PARENT OR CARER INSTALL A WATER STORAGE BARREL, OR JUST LEAVE A BUCKET OUTSIDE TO CATCH THE RAIN. GIVE THE WATER TO THIRSTY PLANTS.

6 DON'T USE A HOSE

Hoses waste water. Use a bucket to wash your car and a watering can to water your plants.

You'll soon find that your water-saving habits become second nature.

GOAL 8

USE LESS ENERGY

There are more people on the planet than ever before, and we're all using more and more energy, which is creating more and more greenhouse gases.

Can you cut down on energy use and achieve this goal?

Unfortunately, almost all the everyday things we do – such as turning on a light, playing video games, and travelling in cars – adds to global warming. This is because we burn fossil fuels, such as gas, oil, or coal, when we generate electricity in power plants, and when we cook, heat our homes, and travel in cars and planes.

THE LARGEST SOURCE OF GREENHOUSE GAS EMISSIONS FROM HUMAN ACTIVITIES IN NORTH AMERICA AND EUROPE IS FROM BURNING FOSSIL FUELS FOR ELECTRICITY, HEAT, AND TRAVEL.

In 2018, 89 percent of the **WHOLE WORLD**'s global-warming carbon dioxide emissions came from burning fossil fuels. The average world temperature has already increased by 2 °F (1 °C), and it's set to get higher if we don't do something about it right now.

THE GOOD NEWS IS THAT MORE AND MORE ENERGY IS RENEWABLE – SUCH AS ELECTRICITY PRODUCED FROM SOLAR PANELS AND WATER AND WIND TURBINES. THESE WAYS OF PRODUCING ENERGY DON'T CREATE GREENHOUSE GAS. AND, UNTIL ALL OUR ENERGY IS RENEWABLE, THERE'S A LOT WE CAN DO TO CUT DOWN!

TOP TIPS TO USE

Turn yourself from an energy-sucking vampire into an energy-saving angel – you'll be saving the planet *and* household energy bills!

1 WATCH FEWER FILMS AND PLAY FEWER VIDEO GAMES

Instead, read a library book, or invite your friends over for a board game. And when you do use your computer or TV, make sure you turn them off when you've finished with them. Leaving a computer on overnight for a year creates enough carbon dioxide to fill a double-decker bus!

2 BEWARE OF "VAMPIRE" APPLIANCES

THESE SUCK ENERGY EVEN WHEN THEY'RE TURNED OFF, SO COMPLETELY UNPLUG YOUR PHONE, LAPTOP, AND TOOTHBRUSH CHARGERS WHEN THEY'RE NOT IN USE.

LESS ENERGY

3 ALWAYS TURN THE LIGHTS OFF WHEN YOU LEAVE A ROOM

A single light left on overnight for a year makes as much greenhouse gas as driving a car from London to Paris!

4 WEAR A WARM SWEATER INSTEAD OF TURNING UP THE HEAT

TURNING THE HEAT DOWN BY JUST 1 ° SAVES 8 PERCENT ON HEATING COSTS, NOT TO MENTION GREENHOUSE GAS EMISSIONS.

5 STOP USING TUMBLE DRYERS

Instead, hang the laundry up outside. Tumble dryers use a lot of electricity – and the wind doesn't use any!

Now you know the facts, tell as many people as you can about what you're doing – then we can all work together to save energy and our planet.

GOAL 9

TAKE GREEN TRANSPORTATION

How do you get about? Do you walk or cycle, or travel in a car, bus, train, or plane?

Humans are traveling more often and much further than ever before, using all sorts of transportation. But ...

TRANSPORTATION BURNS MOST OF THE WORLD'S GASOLINE, PRODUCING 15 PERCENT OF GLOBAL GREENHOUSE GAS EMISSIONS. ENGINE EXHAUSTS ALSO CREATE AIR POLLUTION.

Park all of the world's approximately 1.4 billion cars, trucks, and buses nose to tail and they'd stretch more than one-and-a-half times around the world! And every day new ones are made and bought.

OVER THE PAST 30 YEARS, MORE AND MORE PEOPLE AROUND THE WORLD HAVE BEEN FLYING IN PLANES, WHICH MEANS MORE GREENHOUSE GAS. PLANES ALSO THROW OTHER DANGEROUS GASES AND POLLUTION HIGH INTO OUR ATMOSPHERE, MAKING GLOBAL WARMING EVEN WORSE.

But it's not all doom and gloom. We're switching to electric cars and trains, which don't produce carbon dioxide. And people are realizing that we all need to move from cars and planes to rail and human power!

TOP TIPS TO GET TO YOUR GREEN TRANSPORTATION GOAL

Imagine a world without the roar of road traffic, with greener transportation that doesn't cost the Earth. If we all act together, we can get there!

Do you need to travel in the car to school or the shops? According to research, we could walk or cycle 41 percent of all the car journeys we make! So why not ...

1 WALK IT

Swapping just one car journey a week for walking reduces car traffic levels by at least 10 percent. Plus walking makes us fitter, stronger, and happier! And if walking's not your thing – roller skate, skateboard, scooter, jog, or run!

2 GET ON YOUR BIKE

CYCLING JUST 1 MILE (1.5 KM) A DAY FOR A YEAR COULD SAVE 330 POUNDS (150 KG) OF CARBON DIOXIDE – THAT'S THE SAME AS PLANTING FOUR TREES AND LETTING THEM GROW FOR 10 YEARS!

If you can't walk or cycle:

3 USE BUSES AND TRAINS

Public transportation is usually a greener option than cars.

5 DON'T FLY

Take a train or ferry to your foreign holiday instead. Or travel by train to a beautiful part of your own country.

4 SHARE THE CAR

IF YOU HAVE TO TRAVEL IN A CAR, LESSEN THE CARBON IMPACT BY FITTING IN AS MANY PEOPLE AS POSSIBLE. EVEN BETTER, PERSUADE YOUR PARENT OR CARER TO SWITCH TO AN ELECTRIC CAR.

If you stick to this advice, you'll probably feel much fitter and happier too!

GOAL

10

BECOME A GREEN CAMPAIGNER

What do we want?

A CLEAN, GREEN PLANET!

When do we want it?

NOW!

NOW IT'S TIME FOR THE FINAL STEP – SHARING YOUR ENTHUSIASM AND KNOWLEDGE WITH THE REST OF THE WORLD BY BECOMING A GREEN CAMPAIGNER!

You won't be alone. Greta Thunberg, who began her "School Strike for Climate" when she was just 15, has inspired millions of young people to speak up and take action for the environment. There are plenty of others too ...

UK sisters Ella and Caitlin McEwan, aged nine and seven, set up a petition asking fast-food restaurants to stop putting plastic toys in kids' meals. After they got 400,000 signatures, Burger King and McDonald's listened to the sisters' demands.

SOCCER-LOVING 16-YEAR-OLD KENYAN, LESEIN MUTUNKEI, RAISES AWARENESS OF DEFORESTATION BY PLANTING A TREE FOR EVERY GOAL HE SCORES.

At the age of 13, Aditya Mukarji from India persuaded local cafes and restaurants to stop using plastic straws.

THE **ULLAPOOL SEA SAVERS**, A GROUP OF CAMPAIGNING KIDS IN SCOTLAND, WON THE **INTERNATIONAL OTTER SURVIVAL FUND**'S **OTTER OSCAR** FOR THEIR WORK IN PROTECTING SEA OTTERS AND THEIR LOCAL MARINE ENVIRONMENT.

TOP TIPS TO BECOME

Here are some tips for budding green campaigners:

1 DECIDE WHAT TO WORK ON

Campaign about something you feel passionately about. This could be:

LOCAL – e.g. stopping food waste at school
NATIONAL – e.g. banning pesticides that kill bees
GLOBAL – e.g. raising awareness about endangered animals, such as the Cerrado jaguar, the black rhino, and the polar bear.

2 JOIN ORGANIZATIONS

GET INVOLVED WITH AN ENVIRONMENTAL GROUP, SUCH AS THE **WORLD WILDLIFE FUND** OR **FRIENDS OF THE EARTH**. THEY HELP TO PLAN ACTIVITIES AND PROVIDE RESOURCES AND SUPPORT.

3 FIND PEOPLE TO CAMPAIGN WITH

Ask your friends and family to join you and form a Green Group. Give it a catchy name!

A GREEN CAMPAIGNER

4 TAKE ACTION

HERE ARE SOME WAYS TO DO THINGS FOR YOURSELF:

- ORGANIZE OR JOIN A TRASH OR BEACH CLEAN-UP
- GO TO A DEMO OR PROTEST (WITH GROWN-UPS)
- BLOG AND SHARE INFORMATION ON SOCIAL MEDIA TO RAISE AWARENESS OF ISSUES
- CIRCULATE A PETITION.

5 BE CREATIVE

LET YOUR IMAGINATION RUN RIOT WITH SIGNS, SLOGANS, AND IDEAS FOR CATCHING ATTENTION.

6 CONTACT LOCAL POLITICIANS AND BUSINESS OWNERS TO ASK FOR CHANGE

Handwritten letters, sent through the mail, are a great way to get attention. Meeting people face to face is even better!

7 USE YOUR LOCAL MEDIA

Children's voices really can make a difference. Contact your local newspaper, radio, or TV station, tell them what you're up to, and spread the word.

But most of all, have fun (while doing a lot of good for our planet!).

GLOSSARY

CARBON DIOXIDE – a gas formed when things decompose or burn, and when animals breathe out.

CARBON MONOXIDE – a poisonous gas produced when fossil fuels burn.

CLIMATE CHANGE – changes in the overall temperature of the Earth.

DEFORESTATION – the destruction of large areas of trees.

EMISSION – something that is given off or sent out.

ENVIRONMENT – the air, water, and land where animals and plants live.

EXTINCTION – the dying out or disappearance of a plant or animal from Earth.

EXTREME WEATHER – floods, storms, heatwaves, and drought.

FOOD CHAIN – a network of living things that rely on each other for food.

FOOD MILES – how far food travels from the farm to our plates.

FOSSIL FUEL – a fuel formed from decomposed prehistoric plants and animals, such as coal, gas, and petroleum.

GLOBAL WARMING – the process causing Earth's temperature to rise.

GREENHOUSE GASES – gases in the atmosphere (including carbon dioxide and methane) that trap energy from the sun, stopping it from escaping into space.

LANDFILL – a tip or trash dump where waste is buried.

METHANE – a gas that occurs naturally and as a result of human activities.

MICROPLASTIC – tiny plastic particles less than 5 millimeters in diameter.

ORGANIC – capable of decomposing (breaking down).

OXYGEN – a gas that animals and humans need in order to breathe.

PALM OIL – the most widely used edible vegetable oil in the world.

PESTICIDES – poisons used to kill insects and other animals.

PLANTATION – a large area of land where a single crop is grown.

RECYCLE – turn waste materials into something useful.

RENEWABLE ENERGY (also called **ALTERNATIVE ENERGY**) – energy produced from natural sources that will never run out, such as wind and water.

SINGLE-USE PLASTIC – plastic objects that are used once, then thrown away.

ZERO WASTE – the goal of allowing no trash to be burned, to go to landfills, or into the sea.

FURTHER INFORMATION

WEBSITES:

www.worldwildlife.org – the World Wildlife Fund, an international organization that conserves wildlife and helps endangered species.

https://friendsoftheearth.uk – Friends of the Earth, a worldwide network that campaigns for environmental awareness and change.

https://ecofriendlykids.co.uk – a website for containing information to help explore the natural world and learn about environmental issues.

https://kids.nationalgeographic.com/science/article/green-tips - National Geographic Kids is full of great information about the natural world. This webpage gives tips about what we can do to help nature and lessen the impact of climate change.

BOOKS:

How You Can Save the Planet by Hendrikus van Hensbergen, 2021, Puffin

Kids Fight Climate Change by Martin Dorey, 2021, Walker Books

Zero Waste Kids by Kathryn Kellogg, 2020, Franklin Watts

Earth Heroes by Lily Dyu, 2020, Nosy Crow

Plastic Sucks! You Can Make a Difference by Dougie Poynter, 2019, Macmillan

INDEX